THE MAGIC OF LANGUAGE

Synonyms and Antonyms

straight/angled

wet/slimy

hard/soft

rough/smooth

By Ann Heinrichs

THE CHILD'S WORLD
CHANHASSEN, MINNESOTA

The Child's World

Published in the United States of America by The Child's World®
PO Box 326, Chanhassen, MN 55317-0326
800-599-READ
www.childsworld.com

Photo Credits: Cover/frontispiece: David Aubrey/Corbis; Interior: Corbis: 5 (Yang Liu),
12 (Aaron Horowitz), 18 (Matthias Kulka), 21 (Patrick Giardino), 28 (Charles Gupton);
Getty Images: 9 (The Image Bank/Peter Hince), 22 (Photodisc/Amos Morgan); Getty
Images/Stone: 7 (Trujillo-Paumier), 24 (Catherine Ledner); Getty Images/Taxi: 10 (John
Terence Turner), 15 (Bill Deering); Dennis MacDonald/PhotoEdit: 17.

The Child's World®: Mary Berendes, Publishing Director

Editorial Directions, Inc.: E. Russell Primm, Editorial Director; Katie Marsico,
Project Editor and Line Editor; Matt Messbarger, Editorial Assistant; Susan Hindman,
Copyeditor; Sarah E. De Capua and Lucia Raatma, Proofreaders; Peter Garnham,
Elizabeth Nellums, Olivia Nellums, Daisy Porter, and Will Wilson, Fact Checkers;
Timothy Griffin/IndexServ, Indexer; Cian Loughlin O'Day, Photo Researcher;
Linda S. Koutris, Photo Editor

The Design Lab: Kathleen Petelinsek, Art Direction; Kari Thornborough, Page Production

Library of Congress Cataloging-in-Publication Data
Heinrichs, Ann.
  Synonyms and antonyms / by Ann Heinrichs.
     p. cm. — (The magic of language)
  Includes index.
  ISBN 1-59296-430-3 (lib. bdg. : alk. paper)
  1. English language—Synonyms and antonyms—Juvenile literature. I. Title.
  PE1591.H43 2006
  428.1—dc22   2005004001

Content Adviser:
Kathy Rzany, MA,
Adjunct Professor,
School of Education,
Dominican University,
River Forest, Illinois

TABLE OF CONTENTS

CHAPTER ONE

WHAT IS A SYNONYM?

EXAMPLE

meadow noisy, penny cent? loud? field?

These questions are hard to answer. In fact, they're impossible to answer! Each question asks you to choose between two things. But the two things are the same!

There is a name for these word pairs. They are called synonyms. Look at these pairs of words from each sentence:

penny/cent   **noisy/loud**   **meadow/field**

Synonyms are words that mean the same thing or almost the same thing.

*Is he **happy, joyful,** or **glad?** Is he **resting, lounging,** or **relaxing?**
Is he **yelling, shouting,** or **screaming?** He's all these things!*

Thousands of words have at least one synonym. Just check out these examples:

EXAMPLE

fast/quick	correct/right	hurry/rush	leap/jump
speak/talk	brag/boast	unhappy/sad	happy/glad
near/close	kettle/pot	gift/present	make/build
big/large	little/small	street/road	sick/ill

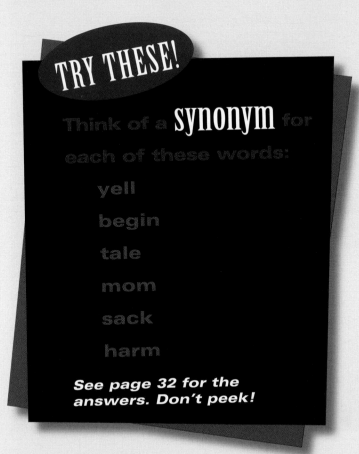

TRY THESE!

Think of a **synonym** for each of these words:

yell

begin

tale

mom

sack

harm

See page 32 for the answers. Don't peek!

Synonyms come in handy. They keep you from repeating yourself. And they help you to tell exciting stories. Let's see what we can do with them!

CHAPTER TWO

GET ATTENTION . . .
NO, GRAB THE SPOTLIGHT!

Do you ever get tired of using the same old words? Why not try using synonyms? An ordinary, everyday word can have really exciting synonyms. Just look at the example on the next page:

He's tired of using the same old words. He needs some synonyms in his life!

Here comes a big dog.
Here comes a huge dog.
Here comes a gigantic dog!

See? A **big** dog is sort of interesting. But a **gigantic** dog is much more exciting! When you hear the word **gigantic,** you begin to wonder about that dog. Is he fierce? Is he friendly? Will he bite?

Here are some more examples of synonyms for ordinary words:

EXAMPLE

ORDINARY WORD	MORE INTERESTING OR EXCITING SYNONYMS
little	tiny, teensy, wee
fast	quick, rapid, speedy, swift
wet	damp, moist, watery
scary	spooky, creepy, terrifying
look	peek, peer, stare, gaze, glance

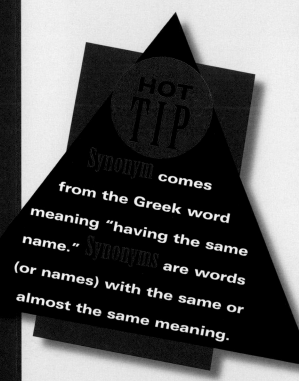

HOT TIP

Synonym comes from the Greek word meaning "having the same name." *Synonyms* are words (or names) with the same or almost the same meaning.

He looking through the magnifying glass. Or maybe he's peering, staring, or gazing through it.

*Is this a **scary** night or a **spooky** night? Are they **cooking** marshmallows or **roasting** them? Are they **telling stories** or **spinning tales?** Good synonyms can make a story much more exciting!*

Next time you **tell** a **story,** use synonyms to **relate** an exciting **tale.** Your story will get attention and put you in the spotlight!

QUICK FACT
A **thesaurus** is a type of dictionary. It lists many **synonyms** for each word.

CHAPTER THREE

DON'T REPEAT, REPEAT, REPEAT!

Ran, ran, ran, ran. Surely this home run was more exciting than that! Why not show the excitement? You can do that by using synonyms for **ran.** Like many words, **ran** has lots of synonyms.

EXAMPLE

I raced to first base, and I darted to
second base.
Then I dashed to third base.
Finally, I sprinted home.

*Cuddles doesn't know what a synonym is. But she knows she doesn't just want to **eat** that goldfish. She wants to **gobble, munch,** and **devour** it!*

Suppose your cat went on an eating spree. You could say:

EXAMPLE

Cuddles ate her cat food.
Then she ate the goldfish.
Next, she ate a few bugs.
For dessert, she ate some flowers.

This hungry kitty is interesting and funny. How can you show that

with words? You can use interesting and funny synonyms for **ate.**

Cuddles gobbled her cat food.
Then she devoured the goldfish.
Next, she munched a few bugs.
For dessert, she nibbled some flowers.

These synonyms paint a much cuter picture of Cuddles. They

really bring her to life. You can almost see her mouth moving!

TRY THESE!

Use **synonyms** to make these sentences more interesting.

1. Sarah **walked** down the hall, **walked** out the door, and **walked** over to the rabbit's cage.

2. Timothy was **happy** when his birthday finally arrived. He was **happy** to eat his cake and **happy** to get a new bike.

3. At the zoo, we saw a **fast** kangaroo, a **fast** zebra, and a **fast** tiger.

See page 32 for the answers. Don't peek!

CHAPTER FOUR

DIFFERENT WORDS FOR DIFFERENT PLACES

Synonyms might have the same meaning. But you can't always exchange one synonym for another. Some words are used mainly when speaking. They may be slang words or sloppy words. They may simply be words that are comfortable to use.

Here are some things you might say when you're speaking:

EXAMPLE

**My sister is always bugging me.
Hoover keeps barking. I wish he would chill.
The guy in the red car has three kids.**

Bugging, chill, guy, and **kids** are informal words.

Sometimes you need to use more formal language. For example, suppose you are giving a speech or writing a report. Then you might use these words instead:

EXAMPLE

My sister is always bothering me.
Hoover keeps barking. I wish he would relax.
The man in the red car has three children.

Do you see the difference between formal and informal words? **Kids** and **children** are synonyms. So are **chill** and **relax.** But they aren't used in exactly the same situations. Each one has its place.

*Informally speaking, Hoover needs to **chill.***
*Formally speaking, he needs to **relax.***

CHAPTER FIVE

TRICKY SYNONYMS

EXAMPLE

I got caught in the rain. My hair is **wet,** and my shirt is **damp.** Even my socks are **moist.**

ook at the three white words in this example. We could use **wet** three times. But that wouldn't be very interesting. Instead, we use the synonyms **damp** and **moist.** All three words are synonyms for one another. Move them around in different places and the meaning stays the same.

Now look at the example on the next page:

Jonathan just left the game.
Now there are only three players left.

The first **left** has a synonym—**departed.** The second **left** also has a synonym—**remaining.** But **departed** and **remaining** are not synonyms. They're almost opposites!

*Her hair is **dripping,** her clothes are **drenched,** and her shoes are* *soaked through and through. In short, she's **wet!***

*The stars are **out** tonight. But what if they went **out**?*

Some words, such as **left,** are tricky. They have two meanings. So they may have two synonyms. But those two synonyms don't mean the same thing at all! Here are some more examples:

WORDS WITH TWO MEANINGS	SYNONYMS
The stars are **out.**	visible
The lights are **out.**	invisible
Have you gone **mad?**	crazy
No, I'm just **mad.**	angry
I **just** finished my homework.	recently
The judge made a **just** decision.	fair
I didn't **mean** to spill the paint.	intend
That monkey is really **mean.**	unkind

CHAPTER SIX

WHAT IS AN ANTONYM?

EXAMPLE

Yesterday I **lost** my iguana, but today I **found** it.

Your snake has **smooth** skin, but my frog has **rough** skin.

In the library we **whisper,** but on the playground we **shout.**

The sun shines all **day,** and the moon shines at **night.**

Look at the pairs of words from the sentences above:

EXAMPLE

lost/found   **smooth/rough**
whisper/shout   **day/night**

There is a name for word pairs like this. They are called antonyms.

19

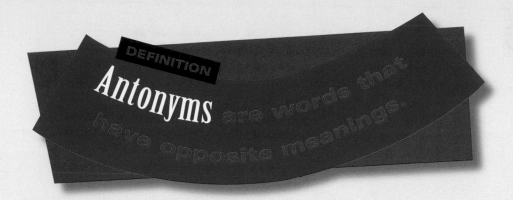

DEFINITION

Antonyms are words that have opposite meanings.

You can probably think of lots of antonyms. Here are just a few:

EXAMPLE

push/pull	high/low
lost/found	true/false
cold/hot	smile/frown
weak/strong	clean/dirty
yes/no	fast/slow
laugh/cry	night/day
work/play	back/front
stop/go	up/down

HOT TIP

Antonym comes from two Greek words. *Ant-* means "against" and *-nym* means "name." Antonyms are words (or names) whose meanings are "against" each other.

20

TRY THESE!

Think of an *antonym* for each of these words:

down   tall
quiet   best
white   less

See page 32 for the answers. Don't peek!

These two basketball players are like antonyms.
*One is **short**, and the other is **tall**.*

CHAPTER SEVEN

USING PREFIXES TO CREATE ANTONYMS

There's an easy way to form antonyms for some words. Just add a prefix that creates the opposite word.

The prefix *un-* changes some words to their opposites. Just look at the next page:

*Is he **buttoning** his shirt? Or is he **unbuttoning** it?*
*It's easy to create antonyms by adding the prefix **un-**.*

I **locked** the bunny's cage and **unlocked** the turtle's pen.

Button your shirt, and **unbutton** your jacket.

The kangaroo was **happy** to escape but was **unhappy** to find no food.

The prefix *dis-* can create antonyms, too.

I **agree** with Derek, but I **disagree** with Peter.

Connect the red wires, and **disconnect** the blue wires.

Judi **likes** chocolate, but she **dislikes** chocolate-covered cherries.

The prefix *non-* also creates antonyms.

Let's use markers with **washable** ink. Markers with **nonwashable** ink will ruin our clothes.

Bushes have **woody** stems, but grasses have **nonwoody** stems.

Badgers are **native** to Wisconsin, but ostriches are **nonnative.**

TRY THESE!

Add a **prefix** to each of these words to create an **antonym:**

tie   respect

expert   like

buckle

See page 32 for the answers. Don't peek!

*Their shoes and bowties are **tied**. But add the prefix **un-**, and they're **untied**!*

CHAPTER EIGHT

USING SUFFIXES TO CREATE ANTONYMS

Now let's learn about a handy pair of suffixes: *-ful* and *-less*. You can use them together to create antonyms. Just look at these examples:

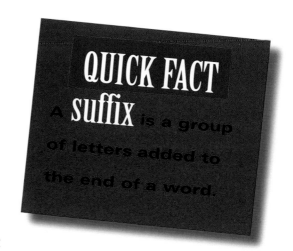

QUICK FACT
A **suffix** is a group of letters added to the end of a word.

EXAMPLE

Cuddles had a **restful** sleep, but Sparky was **restless** all night long.

A spoon is **useful** for eating soup. That fork is **useless**.

Ms. Carter is **fearful** when she sees a mouse. She's **fearless** when she visits the principal, though.

Be **careful** with that goldfish bowl. We don't want any **careless** spills!

CHAPTER NINE

ANTONYMS IN PROVERBS

Have you heard of proverbs? Proverbs are wise sayings that teach a lesson. Some proverbs have existed for hundreds of years!

Proverbs are usually short. This helps people to remember them easily. Many proverbs use antonyms, too. They put opposite ideas together. That makes people sit up and think!

Here's a proverb you might know:

EXAMPLE

All work and no play make Jack a dull boy.

This proverb uses the antonyms **work** and **play.** What lesson does it teach? It teaches that it's not good to do just one activity all the time. This wears out your mind!

Look at the next page for another good proverb:

One person's trash is another person's treasure.

Trash and **treasure** are antonyms. At first, you might wonder how this proverb can be true. But just think: You might collect comic books but throw baseball cards away. Your friend might collect baseball cards but throw marbles away. Another person might collect marbles but throw comic books away!

The proverb uses antonyms to teach a good lesson: Everyone has different needs, wishes, and values.

TRY THESE!

Pick out the **antonyms** in these proverbs. What do you think each proverb means?

1. Great oaks from little acorns grow.
2. You can't teach an old dog new tricks.
3. Don't make a mountain out of a molehill.

See page 32 for the answers. Don't peek!

CHAPTER TEN

TRICKY ANTONYMS

Nicki and Tricky are friends. Tricky knows that some words are tricky—just like he is. These words are tricky because they have two antonyms. He uses tricky antonyms to confuse his friend Nicki. On the next page, see how he does it!

*The exam is really **hard**. Her friend said to try a **soft** one instead. But she's not amused. She's not in the mood for tricky antonyms today!*

NICKI: This exam is too **hard!**

TRICKY: Then take a **soft** exam instead.

NICKI: Did Emily make a **right** turn at the corner?

TRICKY: No, she made a **wrong** turn.

NICKI: I'm starving. I've been **fasting** since midnight.

TRICKY: Then try **slowing** down.

No wonder Nicki is confused! Some words have two antonyms. That's because those words have two meanings. Nicki is thinking of one meaning. But Tricky is thinking of the other meaning. Here are some words with two meanings and two antonyms:

EXAMPLE

right/left	**right/wrong**
light/dark	**light/heavy**
hard/easy	**hard/soft**
fast/eat	**fast/slow**

Can you think of other ways to use tricky antonyms?

How to Learn More

At the Library

Félix, Monique. *The Opposites.* Makato, Minn.: Creative Education, 1992.

Marron, Carol A., and Cindy Wheeler (illustrator). *Someone Just like Me.* Milwaukee: Raintree Publishers, 1983.

Pittau, Francisco, and Bernadette Gervais. *Elephant Elephant: A Book of Opposites.* New York: Harry N. Abrams, 2001.

Swinburne, Stephen R. *What's Opposite?.* Honesdale, Penn.: Boyds Mill Press, 2000.

Wilbur, Richard. *More Opposites.* Harcourt: New York, 1991.

On the Web

Visit our home page for lots of links about grammar:
http://www.childsworld.com/links

NOTE TO PARENTS, TEACHERS AND LIBRARIANS: We routinely check our Web links to make sure they're safe, active sites—so encourage your readers to check them out!

Through the Mail or by Phone

To find the answer to a grammar question, contact:

THE GRAMMAR HOTLINE DIRECTORY
Tidewater Community College Writing Center, Building B205
1700 College Crescent
Virginia Beach, VA 23453
Telephone: (757) 822-7170

NATIONWIDE GRAMMAR HOTLINE
University of Arkansas at Little Rock, English Department
2801 South University Avenue
Little Rock, AR 72204-1099
Telephone: (501) 569-3161

Fun with Synonyms and Antonyms

Match each word in column A with its synonym in column B.

A	B
1. fast	hurry
2. rush	hurt
3. happy	piece
4. harm	correct
5. shiny	happiness
6. part	glad
7. right	quick
8. joy	bright

Match each word in column A with its antonym in column B.

A	B
1. day	tight
2. soft	harmless
3. loose	go
4. work	night
5. harmful	quiet
6. stop	thick
7. thin	hard
8. loud	play

See page 32 for the answers. Don't peek!

Index

Answers

Answers to Text Exercises
page 6
Some possible answers are:
shout, start, story, mother, bag, hurt.

page 13
Some possible answers are:
1. ambled, marched, pranced, sauntered, shuffled
2. delighted, glad, overjoyed, pleased, thrilled
3. quick, racing, speedy, swift

page 21
Some possible answers are:
up, short, loud, worst, black, more

page 24
untie, disrespect, nonexpert, dislike, unbuckle

page 27
1. (great/little) Any large project begins with small steps.
2. (old/new) Those who have long-held habits do not learn new ways easily.
3. (mountain/molehill) Don't make a big deal out of something unimportant.

Answers to Fun with Synonyms and Antonyms

Synonyms	Antonyms
1. fast/quick	1. day/night
2. rush/hurry	2. soft/hard
3. happy/glad	3. loose/tight
4. harm/hurt	4. work/play
5. shiny/bright	5. harmful/harmless
6. part/piece	6. stop/go
7. right/correct	7. thin/thick
8. joy/happiness	8. loud/quiet

About the Author

Ann Heinrichs was lucky. Every year from grade three through grade eight, she had a big, fat grammar textbook and a grammar workbook. She feels that this prepared her for life. She is now the author of more than 180 books for children and young adults. She has also enjoyed successful careers as a children's book editor and an advertising copywriter. Ann grew up in Fort Smith, Arkansas, and lives in Chicago, Illinois.